1

**Cover Photo
Courtesy of
Frank Simkonis**

Copyright 2015 Nancy Orlando
All rights reserved. No part of this publication may be reproduced,
stored in a retrieval system, or transmitted in any form or by any means,
electronic, mechanical, photocopying or otherwise, without
the written prior permission of the author.

Printed in the United States of America
ISBN 10-0990559912
ISBN 13-978-0-9905599-1-7

GOD'S HILL

A History of love and stewardship

By Nancy Orlando

CONTENTS

Cover Photo Credit..................................Page 1

Copyright page...Page 2

Title Page..Page 3

Contents...Page 4

Dedication..Page 5

Forward..Page 6

Chapter 1.........Creation...........................Page 11

Chapter 2.........Wine................................Page 17

Chapter 3.........Stone Houses..................Page 29

Chapter 4.........Church Attendance.........Page 40

Chapter 5.........Religious Progress..........Page 43

Summary..Page 54

Post Script...Page 55

St. Joseph in the Hills (poem)..................Page 56

Special People..Page 57

End Notes...Page 59

DEDICATION

This book is dedicated to you, the remarkable people and wonderful children of Camp Springs, Kentucky. I have tried to stitch together the scattered pieces of your history so your story is available for all. I want readers of history to know how very special your community is.

The year I have spent getting to know you and your ancestors has been an inspiration to me and has created memories I will cherish.

Thank you.

FORWARD

This book is the result of a chance meeting with Mike Enzweiler at my daughter's antique and gift shop. The gifts in her shop were created by local craftsmen and artists. The artists were there to meet and greet customers. I was there to display my children's books.

Mike, a local artist, told me about St. Joseph School in Camp Springs. In this day of tight budgets preventing classes in the arts, this school invites artists and craftsmen, who wish to donate their time, once each month, to discuss their particular form of art and introduce the children to a new artistic expression. Mike said he would tell the school that my illustrator and I would be available to read one of our books to the school. I had lived on Four Mile Road many years before. The garden in my book "A Garden! A Garden!" was our garden on top of the hill behind our house, so I had a connection to these children and this school.

Beautiful mural was painted by Paula Edwards.

My illustrator, Debbi Kern, and I read to every child in the school, grades K through 8, all 32 of them!

I had read about the school on their site and learned that the school had been in continuous operation since 1851, ten years before the Civil War. Children in the area were gathered in one home and taught by the local priest until a log cabin was built to house a school. Being a writer I immediately saw a book in this history. As the day progressed I learned about the struggles and commitment of these people to keep this school open.

Yours truly, Mike Enzweiler and Theresa Averbeck

Theresa Averbeck worked with us to set up our reading. She has been with the school for over twenty years as the volunteer librarian. Talk about commitment!

Mike's dedication is also inspiring. His art projects appear on the school grounds from time to time to delight and inspire.

Everyone at the school, teacher or student, is represented on one of the arrows

Sometimes the inspiration is just a good laugh! Mike organized the Visiting Artist series, bringing someone to show and discuss a new art form once each month. From this the children learn to understand and appreciate various forms of art.

The school has survived in spite of many crisis. I learned that some years certain grades or classes were not taught due to financial restraints. There was currently a drive to have a preschool class. Again, the financial burden of such a class was being weighed. I left the school that day determined to find a way to help them. At the bottom of the drive, we stopped to take a picture.

Someone behind us stopped to be sure we were all right. We told her we wanted a picture to show how high the hill with church and school on top was. She told us some locals refer to it as God's Hill. I knew that would be the title of the book I would write. It would be the history and stewardship of God's Hill from the time of creation.

I called Mike to tell him of my idea for a book they could sell to bring in revenue for the school. He arranged for me to meet with local residents who would share historical data with me. That meeting was informative, but I needed more information. I found the Baumann files.

This lengthy research on the genealogy of the first settlers had the information I needed. This material would allow me to write the book I had in mind. I found an email address for the researcher and sent an email introducing myself and my plan for the book. Mr. Baumann kindly gave me permission to use his material. He has answered questions and provided additional material. I cannot thank him enough. Without his commitment to writing this history, this book could never be written.

I am not a historian. I need facts to glean a story from. As I studied Mr. Baumann's work, I was excited to find in those early settlers that same palpable sense of pride, the can-do spirit and commitment that I felt so strongly at the school. Finally, I was prepared to begin the story of the history and stewardship of God's Hill!

GOD'S HILL

Chapter One

Creation

In the beginning............................I can only imagine God looking over his beautiful creation. In a place that would remain undeveloped and undiscovered, a beautiful hill stood out in the rolling countryside. It was obvious this hill was special, but it would take man and many millennium to determine how it would be special.

God created man, and slowly the world was populated and discovered. The first humans to occupy the area around God's Hill were the American Indians of the Fort Ancient Period, 1000 to 1600 A.D. Archeologists have discovered these forerunners of the Shawnee lived in the Twelve Mile Creek watershed.

Various Indian cultures fought over the "Great Meadow" that would become Kentucky, but none ever claimed possession of the land. They fought for the right to hunt the abundant wild life and gather the fruits, nuts and edible foods that grew in this special place.

Meanwhile, man was populating the world God had created and began to invent things to make life easier. He began to explore. In 1492 Columbus arrived in America and by the mid 1500's explorers were roaming the rivers and mountains of this new land. Hernando De Soto traveled through this area in 1541. In the 1600's colonies were founded in Virginia and in 1620 the pilgrims arrived at Plymouth Rock.

By the 1700's, the rolling hills around God's Hill were part of Virginia. In 1772 the county of Fincastle, Virginia was formally divided into Washington, Montgomery and Kentucky Counties. After the Revolutionary War the counties beyond the Appalachians became known as Kentucky.

The word Kentucky is a corruption of the Wyandot word kah-ten-tah-the, meaning a day. Shortened to Ken-tah-teh it means "tomorrow". Gradually, it became the word applied to the land south of the Ohio River. This meant "the land of tomorrow" or "the land where we will go tomorrow" or "the land where we will live in the future." The word was easily corrupted by settlers. Ken-tah-teh became Contocky or Cantuckee or Kaintuckee and finally Kentucky – "the land of tomorrow."

In 1783, God's Hill and the surrounding rolling land were part of a 500 acre patent that was awarded to Isaac Ware. He was also granted two warrants for land. Warrant 16460 gave him 883 acres and warrant 16773 gave him another 861 acres. Acquiring large tracts of land by warrants or patents was a good investment for anyone who believed the settlers would continue to come and need to buy acreage to farm and build homes.

The settlers who lived in Kentucky County wanted separation from Virginia. Travel to the capital was long and dangerous, plus Virginia refused to understand the need for commerce on the Mississippi River to trade with New Orleans. Such trade was forbidden. The growing population faced constant conflicts with the Native Americans. The settlers felt Virginia did not adequately protect them. Some thought the new federal government was weak and wanted to declare themselves to be an independent nation. Others who saw the need for trade with Spanish held New Orleans as a reason for an alliance with Spain. They convened their first Constitutional Convention in 1784. Nine more conventions followed. On June 1, 1792, under terms agreed to by all parties, without ever being declared a territory, Kentucky became the 15th state.

By the 1840's settlers from Germany and Austria left their homes to settle in the hills surrounding God's Hill, then known as the Four Mile area. They came from the Saar region along the border of Germany, France and Luxembourg. Mostly Catholic, the area of Germany was sometimes known as Prussia or Rhineland. Unemployment and serious crop failures lead to a major famine in the entire area. Hunger riots and violent disturbances were frequent events. Many left a record in the church records of their home village in Germany. Others escaped into France to avoid being called into the service of the Monarch. This was felt to be an unjust control of the lower class of farmers. They came to America to avoid all these problems, practice their faith and pass their way of life on to their children.

That trip was fraught with problems. Passage was not cheap, nor was it comfortable. For those who could afford the price, there were a few cabins available. For a bit less they could occupy the open spaces below deck which gave them some protection from the elements. The least expensive and commonly used way was simply to sit on the deck. They used blankets or whatever they could improvise to protect themselves from the elements.

Picture from archives at Ellis Island.

Imagine these people on a stormy day!

None of the fares included meals. It was recommended that each family provide a potato per person per day. They literally lived on potato soup during that long voyage! There is no way we can appreciate the strength of even the frailest among them for what they endured to have a chance for a new life for themselves and for us, their heirs.

In 1841, a group of 21 left Germany for the new world. Peter Steffen, age 59, came with the children from his second marriage. There were twelve in his family group. Peter Steffen, age 30, and his wife Maria Gaspar, brought their three children. Mathias Steffen, age 27, had four in his group.

In July of 1843 Michael Enzweiler and Mathias Kremer left their church and town in Germany on the same day. They came to the port of New Orleans. The Enzweiler family moved up the Mississippi and Ohio Rivers and joined the settlers in Four Mile. The Kremers remained in New Orleans for two years before moving north to the Four Mile area.

On that same boat to New Orleans was the family of Nicholas Blau. Nicholas was 53 years old and his wife Katherin was 50. Their children aged 11, 9, 7, and 3 arrived with them to call this new place in America home.

On June 27, 1846, Jacob Frederick Walter, emigrated from the Baden region in Germany, bound for New Orleans. He is believed to have been a grape grower. His 1899 headstone at St. John's Lutheran Cemetery in Camp Springs has a grape cluster on it.

That original patent for 500 acres to Isaac Ware may have changed hands but in 1841, the elder Steffen acquired 62 acres of that original land from a Richard Southgate. The land was in Four Mile, which we know today as Camp Springs. Michael Enzweiler also bought a large tract adjoining the Steffen land. The new settlers were pleased that the rolling hills were perfect for growing grapes. They were also pleased with the abundance of surface limestone rocks that could be used for the construction of walls and homes. The most desirable land was taken so they were forced to settle on hillsides and valleys. Since most came from hillside farms and wine regions along the Rhine River in Germany, they had the skills they would need.

There were, of course, those who were too dedicated to leave the homeland. They were all honest people who would dedicate themselves to the land they chose to call home.

Years later, this led to heartbreak for the same family on two sides of the same war. (In Don Bauman's words)

"Albert Enzweiler of the German Army gave his life for his country, May 5, 1945.

Albert Enzweiler of Alexandria, KY – US Army also gave his life for his country on the beach at Sicily in 1944.

Did either family grieve less? I think not."

Grotto (soldiers War Memorial) built by parishioners after St. Joseph's lost a soldier on the beaches of Italy in 1944.

GOD'S HILL

Chapter Two

Wine

Some of the early settlers came to the port of New Orleans. They came up the Mississippi and the Ohio Rivers. When they reached Cincinnati they found their way to the promising farmlands and the kinship of the earlier settlers in Four Mile.

They planted grapes and tended the vines which produced more fruit each year. We have no records of the wine production, so we can only assume how the process was done. When the grapes were gathered, they were probably removed from the stems by hand. It was much too early for crusher and destemming equipment. A basket press would have been used to extract the juice. The juice was allowed to settle for at least a day. Then it was moved to large vats or kettles to ferment. A cool location was needed for this process. A number of the stone houses had vaulted cellars which were perfect for maintaining cool temperatures. White wines were fermented in closed containers, so no oxygen mixed in with the juice and damaged the wine. Red wine, in contrast, benefited from oxygen. It was fermented in open top vessels.

Kentucky's and America's commercial wine industry was born in 1798. Jean- Jacques Defour, the winemaker of Marquis de Lafayette, looked for suitable land for growing grapes. In Lexington, he met Henry Clay.

Backed with money from several statesmen including Clay, Defour formed the Kentucky Vineyard Society and bought 600 acres on the Kentucky River in what is now Jessamine County. He planted what he called the "First Vineyard." In 1803, his first vintage went to an appreciative President Thomas Jefferson.

In the 1840's, Cincinnatian, Nicholas Longworth saw opportunity in the Ohio River Valley's southward facing slopes and broad waters. The early growers and vintners called the area "The Rhineland of America," because the Ohio River Valley was so similar to the Rhine River Valley, the region responsible for fine wines in Germany and the homeland of so many of the settlers. At the time, President Thomas Jefferson was pushing vineyard planting in America, predicting America's first agricultural success would be from the grape.

Longworth, a very early commercial Vintner, produced "Pure Catawba" wines that were winning blue ribbons at local fairs. In 1842, he accidentally developed a Sparkling Catawba wine that could compete with old world champagne. When his attempts to duplicate it failed, he sent for a French wine maker. Finally in 1847 he found a successor who had experience crafting similarly made champagnes. This new sparkling Catawba product expanded wine making in America to an industry.

In 1848, Longworth wrote "I have for the past five years, believed that the land in Kentucky, on the opposite side of the Ohio, would be preferable for the grape culture, to our own. The soil on that side of the river is in many situations sandy, and the rain forces freely through it."

Later that year, while on a tour of vineyards upriver from Cincinnati, he reported:

"This day I visited a German settlement on the Ohio, commencing about twelve miles above the city, and extending about four miles. The hill commences close to the river, and rises gradually; the usual bottomland being on the opposite (Ohio) side of the river......nearly the whole of the four miles is occupied by vineyards, and there are also some on top of the hill. Two of the vineyards belong to Englishmen, the owners of all the others are German."

His account, unmistakably describing Camp Springs, offers a rare glimpse into the German character of the community. It also shows that the Germans, by mid-century had developed an agricultural economy that deviated from other regions in the state and nation. Campbell County and Camp Springs produced one-third of the national output of wine. It registered the fewest number of slaves and slave-owners of all Kentucky counties with valuable land. Farms were relatively small, reflecting the absence of a slave economy. In 1860 for example, over 800 of the county's 1100 farms contained less than 50 acres. Only two of the German owned farms in Camp Springs encompassed over 100 acres.

Wine making flourished until the early 1860's. Rot and mildew disease ravaged the vineyards. None of the known treatments worked on this new strain of the disease.

Vines died leaving the settlers to find a new way to survive. They adapted and raised food crops and animals to take to Covington and Cincinnati markets.

Roads during this time were nothing more than trails along creeks or wagon wheel ruts in more traveled areas. It was impossible to travel without passing over land belonging to others. According to the Baumann history a few toll houses were erected so tolls could be collected by the land owners.

During this period The Civil War occurred. Sentiments in Four Mile were strongly pro Union, but the area was rural and remote, so it was not deeply affected by the War. Records show that many residents from Campbell County, who were not yet U.S. citizens served in the Union Army. At Wars end they received their citizenship papers, some signed by General Ulysses S. Grant.

It is said that during the war a squad of Union soldiers camped beside Four Mile Creek in the valley. The name Camp Springs came into being at that time.

Even though the blight of the 1880's destroyed most of the vines. Prohibition in the 1920's ended what was left of the wine industry but the lure of the vine remained. Tobacco became the main cash crop of Kentucky, but vineyards and wine making never lost favor with Kentucky farmers.

Dennis Walter owns the farm acquired by his great-great-grandfather in the 1840's. In 1871 Charles Walter ran a blacksmith shop from a huge barn on the property. He repaired metal hardware for local farmers and manufactured coaches and wagons. Several hay wagons produced in that era remain on the farm today

In 2001, Dennis and his wife Bonnie returned to their roots, growing grapes. In 2005 they opened a winery and tasting room to celebrate the fruits of their labor: making commercial wine. They also prepare bar-b-que dinners with wine tastings several times each month and host several B&B wine cruises during the summer months.

    This renovated 1890 farmhouse has been converted into a cozy wine tasting room. The small summer kitchen, smokehouse and outbuilding provide a glimpse into the lifestyle of the early inhabitants. Many of the tools and household items used in the late 1800's are on display in the tasting room.

    The original Walter home located beside the winery was built 1871. It is on the National Historic Register.

In 2005, Lonnie Enzweiler had 53 acres sitting idle, that he had no plans to use. His son Chris suggested they start a vineyard. Lonnie agreed and 200 Vidal Blanc vines were planted. A year later, a second field was cleared and 650 additional vines were planted.

In 2007 the first crop was harvested from field one and Five Waters Road was cut to allow better access to the upper fields. The following year, field three was cleared. Nine hundred Cabernet Franc vines were set.

Lonnie's other son, Kevin wanted to use the grapes for a family wine business. Construction of Camp Springs Winery and tasting room was begun. That year over 2,000 pounds of grapes were harvested from field one.

In 2015 a new kitchen was completed to begin serving dinners. A fourth field was cleared and planted to continue the growth of this small family winery.

Harvest time is family time at Camp Springs Winery. They pick the grapes and then remove the grapes from the stems just as the early pioneers did before the invention of destemming equipment.

The resurgence of wine in Northern Kentucky, has partly been made possible by grants from the Kentucky Department of Agriculture to aid farmers to diversify away from tobacco as a state cash crop. Virginia was first to employ state Extension specialists to research and educate local farmers on the possibility of growing grapes. Seeing success, Northern Kentucky farmers jumped on board, gathering information from other regional resources and planting vines locally – some in the same terraces where grapes were grown over a century ago.

The University of Kentucky Cooperative Extension Service supports the commercial wine producers, employing full-time researchers and field technicians to assist vine dressers and vintners. There is now a state-wide council serving nearly fifty vineyards and wineries in Kentucky, which sponsors a state-wide wine trail and tourism program. Since the turn of the century, Kentucky has grown from 67 to over 500 acres in vineyard production. Kentucky wine is selling approximately 100,000 cases of wine per year.

The rebirth of the wine industry is returning the rolling hills around God's Hill to the tranquil beauty of a century ago.

There is another family farm that has stayed in the family since the 1840's. It isn't a vineyard or a winery but it is land that has supported 6 generations of the same family.

The Clarence Neltner family currently stewards the Neltner Farm and Greenhouses on Four Mile Road. They are the current generation of the heirs of Joseph Neltner who arrived in 1845 from Germany with his wife, Rosina.

The farm had evolved into a dairy farm until 1976 when the family decided to diversify to provide fresh homegrown produce to the area. For the past 20 years they have used greenhouses to raise hydroponic vegetables. Tomatoes are market ready as early as May.

The greenhouses provide plants in the spring, followed by fields of strawberries, tomatoes and vegetables. Flower baskets and homemade goodies fill in until the fall berries, peaches and apples are ripe. Pumpkins mean it is time for the fall festival on weekends in October. That's the

time to bring the children to enjoy a fun time at the farm with the animals.

The Neltners also host weddings and special occasions on the picturesque farm.

During the growing season, you will find them with their produce at various farmer's markets including the Campbell County market on Tuesdays.

Saturdays you will find them at the historic Findlay Market in Cincinnati.

GOD'S HILL

Chapter Three

STONE HOUSES

Stone foundations and stone houses are not uncommon in Germany. The early settlers brought with them the skills to build walls and homes from the native rock. Unfortunately, we have no accounts about the actual building of these homes. Many questions come to mind that cannot be answered. We don't know how long it took to build one. It must have been months, perhaps years.

Did they put all the rocks in a community area or did each family have a rock pile at the site for their home? We know rocks were collected from river and creek beds and from the cleared land. Every rain uncovered more limestone rocks. I am told, just inches below the surface in many areas, one can find layers of limestone, four to six inches thick.

While the rocks were being gathered, temporary homes were log or simple frame buildings. One family built the barn and lived in it so they could begin to clear and farm the land. Some of the families were capable of building a rock home but many of the homes show signs of a particular craftsman. Nicholas Reitman was one such craftsman. His skills and particular building methods are obvious in several of the homes. The structures give a special character and charm to the Camp Springs area. Twenty six of these homes are on the National Register.

A listing on The National Register of Historic Places means a property has been confirmed to be worthy of preservation. Careful consideration should be given to these properties to maintain their historic character and integrity. It is truly astonishing for a community as small as Camp Springs to have so many homes listed.

The Camp Springs homes are unique. They follow a more European design with German roots. The stone is considered to be rubble stone. The builders were artisans who fit the stones into intricate patterns. On the other hand, the stone homes in central Kentucky show more refined hand hewn rocks. This special rock preparation was possible due to the slave economy of that area.

The Camp Springs home of Isidore Baumann, the great grandfather of our historian/geneologist Don Baumann was probably built prior to 1850. The census that year, appraised Baumann's real estate at a high figure. He lived in the home until the late 1800's.

(Photo courtesty of Mark A Ramler)

The Nicholas Kremer House was completed in 1868. Nicholas was the brother of Frederick and Mathias. The house has a somewhat different setting than the other stone houses. It sits back from the road.

(Photo by Don Weideman 2008)

Notice the beautiful stone wall. This one was rebuilt within the past 15 years. It is true to the original walls built in the 1800's. Many of these historical walls were lost in the late 1920's, when roads in the area were improved. Rock walls were pushed to the roadway to be crushed into gravel.

Rock Crusher at work

Photo courtesy of NKY views.com

Enough beautiful rock walls were crushed to create 38 miles of gravel roads

(Information provided by Mark A. Ramler)

Blau's Four Mile House was probably built by Nicholas Reitman and Stephen Blau. Banked construction was a very common German solution to building in hilly terrain. Tax records in 1875 show that Stephen Blau held a tavern license. Bank construction gave access to the tavern on the lower level and access by a rear second story entrance to the living area.

Adjacent to this house is a small bank barn built into the hillside with a limestone foundation and retaining walls between the house and the barn.

(Photo Courtesy of Mark A. Ramler)

The Camp Springs House is one of the most impressive stone buildings in the area. Built in the 1860's for William Uthe by the Ort brothers, it took about four years to build. It has been a stagecoach stop, a tavern, an inn and also the Indian Springs post office. The second floor once had a dance hall and a card room. It was also popular for its beer garden and horseshoe tournaments.

There is a vaulted cellar built into the hillside which is now covered by a porch. It was used to store wine and spirits produced in the area and maintains a constant temperature of 52 degrees. The structure is currently used as a bed and breakfast. (Photo courtesy of Mark A. Ramler)

There are three round smokehouses remaining in Camp Springs. This one on the Hilbert farm appears to have its original standing seam metal roof.

Photo by Don Weideman 2008

This smokehouse is surrounded by Reitman's Auto Parts but is highly visible due to its proximity to the road. The roof has been replaced and would have originally been a standing seam metal one like the one on the Hilbert farm. It is currently used as an information stop on the annual Stone House Trail.

(Courtesy of Mark A. Ramler)

You get a perfect night's sleep in a stone house during a storm. There simply isn't a sound that can penetrate through two foot thick walls (note window sill depth).

It's like a fortress. You have to feel secure within these beautiful stone walls. The heat retention in winter and the coolness in summer offer year round comfort.

(Photos courtesy of photographer Frank Simkonis)

Built of brick, made on the premises, The Weber Dairy Farm has been an impressive sight since it was built in 1852. John Weber migrated from Germany through New Orleans. Some think the architecture there inspired him to build this Greek Revival Mansion. It sits on a limestone foundation that employs vaulted ceilings similar to other Camp Springs cellars.

(Photo courtesy of Mark A. Ramler)

This is an example of a vaulted cellar as the one described under The Weber Dairy. These cellars were excellent for storing perishable goods. They maintained steady temperatures, usually around 52 degrees Fahrenheit.

(Photo Courtesy of Mark A. Ramler)

Don Baumann arranged this collage of Camp Springs doors and sent it to me. I think it is a perfect ending for the chapter on the homes of Camp Springs.

God's Hill

Chapter Four

Church Attendance

There was one great negative to life in this new world. There was no Catholic Church close enough for regular attendance. The settlers had to make the long trip to Covington or Cincinnati to attend church and receive the sacraments. This meant church was a rare occurrence. Whenever a celebrant was available, the settlers gathered in the Steffen home or the Michael Enzweiler home for Mass. They petitioned the Bishop in Louisville to send a priest at least on special occasions. The closest priest lived in Newport. The twelve mile hike made it impossible for him to come often enough to satisfy the spiritual needs of the congregation. The members raised ten dollars to buy a horse he could ride to Camp Springs. The arrangement with the horseback riding priest from Newport continued for six years.

The parishioners were encouraged to build a small church. Peter Steffen gave one half acre of land to be used to build the church. The other families collected $10 to buy the adjoining half acre to add to the church land.

During December 1845 and January and February of 1846 the best trees were cut and the logs were prepared. On March 24, 1846 the settlers came together and erected the 35 by 50 foot building in a single day.

The interior of the church was completed over the next two months and was placed under the patronage of St. Joseph.

With the church completed, many things were still needed, such as vestments, a chalice and other sacred vessels for the altar. In 1848, the men of the parish, married and single, organized a society to raise the funds to provide and maintain these necessities. The first officers of this society were Michael Enzweiler, Andrew Blenke and Isidore Bauman. Each member pledged ten cents monthly so these needs could be easily met.

In 1845, while the settlers were preparing the logs for the new church, Joseph Neltner with his new wife, Rosina Ruschman Neltner arrived at the port of New York. With them came Rosina's mother, Katherina Ruschman, her brother, Ignatius Ruschman with his wife Mary Ursula Speier, Mary's sister, Rosalia Speier and husband Karl Antone Kubel. Three nieces also came to America with them. The Neltner family came to Northern Kentucky to join the other German immigrants who bought farms and built homes in America. Sadly, Rosina's mother became ill during the trip and died soon after arriving in Kentucky. Not all attempts to find a new life had happy endings.

Soon after arriving in Northern Kentucky, Rosalia and Karl Kubel traveled to Indiana and made their home there. Ignatius Ruschman settled with his family in what is now called Wilder, Kentucky. Joseph and Rosina Neltner lived in a log cabin in Wilder until they moved to Ross,

Kentucky. It was in the census district known as Indian Springs which included the Camp Springs area.

The Neltner family became prominent in Northern Kentucky in spite of tragedy. Joseph's wife, Rosina died in 1861, leaving him with a son, Joseph, and a new infant. He was unable to care for them so they were taken to the Kubel relatives in Indiana. The baby died at the age of two months. Joseph, now 39, remarried shortly after Rosina's death.

He married 24 year-old Katherina Steffen. She was born in Germany, but came to America and lived with her parents in Camp Springs. She was 15 years younger than Joseph but was considered a likely mother for his children. After their marriage, Little Joseph was brought from Indiana to be reunited with his family and his new mother. Joseph built a large barn and a six room brick home on his farm in Ross, Kentucky. They soon filled the home with nine additional children. Before his death in 1899, Joseph owned seven farms in Campbell County. Some of these farms were worked by his sons' families until they too became property owners.

In 1846, just after the arrival of the Neltners, John Peter Steffen and his family emigrated from Bachem, Germany. Wilhelm Steffen and his family arrived from Losheim in 1852. In just a little over 10 years, the entire living family of Peter Steffen joined him in America. Imagine the thrill and excitement of that family being reunited in one place to face the future together.

GOD'S HILL

Chapter Five

Religious Progress

In 1851 Rev. John Voll was appointed Pastor, which elevated St. Joseph in the Hills from a mission congregation to a full fledged parish.

Rev. John Voll

He began immediately to educate the children. After his daily Mass he gathered the children in one of the homes and spent most of the day teaching.

The number of children grew steadily and soon the homes were too small to hold classes.

Father Voll worked to build a log cabin to house the school. The first school was a tiny log cabin erected near the church. The patch of land it sat on, is now part of St. Joseph Cemetery.

There were sixty five families that were members of St Joseph church in 1853 when Bishop Spaulding of Louisville, Kentucky visited. The families were almost entirely of German heritage.

Over the next ten years membership in the parish grew. The community of Alexandria separated from St. Joseph and formed St. Mary parish. St. Peter and Paul parish and Immaculate Conception Mission were formed in Twelve Mile and Stepstone.

Earlier, around 1856, Father Stephan had purchased ten acres which included God's Hill, from Mathias and Margaret Kremer for $600. With the arrival of Reverend Eberhard Schulte in July of 1864, completion of a new church became a priority. Contracts were given for the brick work and carpentry.

A place to make the bricks for the church was set up along the creek behind the Baumann farm near the bottom of the hill. The community once again came together to produce the bricks for a new church building. The bricks would have been made from clay dug around the creek and sandy mud from the creek bed. Water from the creek provided the necessary mixing ingredient. No records of the actual brick making have come down to us. We can only assume they used the same brick making methods as the early settlers in Williamsburg. They probably built a pit to mix the clay, sand and water and possibly mixed in dried grass or straw to bind the mixture. It's true that stomping with bare feet is an excellent way to blend the mix. If they followed this tried and true method, the children would have been a great asset for this boring job. While the job was boring, I'm sure the children would have been delighted to be part of such an important project in such a messy manner!

The resulting mix was pressed into wooden forms. The wet brick was then gently dumped out to dry in the sun. The bricks had to be turned frequently to dry evenly. When they were dry enough to move they would have been moved to a shady area to dry to a state solid enough to fire in pits built along the creek.

To prepare the pits, unfired bricks were laid to enclose a 2 or 3 square foot area. Layers were added, leaving a quarter inch space between bricks for air to circulate. The layers continued to a height of two or three feet. A large sheet of metal would have covered the top of the kiln. The dried bricks surrounded by fire wood were placed in the kiln and the wood was set on fire. The metal top was kept in place during the firing which had to be kept burning for at least six days and nights. After firing, the bricks cooled for a week before they could be used.

The current resident of the property says the area is still littered with broken bricks and more are exposed any time digging in the area occurs.

The unbounded determination and commitment of the settlers took them through the arduous task of making the bricks, drying them and building the kilns to fire them in. That was, however, just the beginning. After all the back breaking work of creating the bricks, they still had to load them, one by one, onto horse drawn carts and wagons for the long dangerous trek up the steep hillside of God's Hill to the site for the new church.

The new structure, 70 feet by 40 feet and 26 feet high was built at a cost of $7,000. It took one and one half years to build.

A delightful bonus was found when the church was completed. They discovered they had just enough bricks left to build a small tavern at the bottom of the hill! It would be a gathering place for the men to socialize and enjoy the wine and beer they would store there.

(From photo by Steve Gordon 1982)

The location for the church was the most commanding point in the entire area at an elevation of about 100 feet above the valley floor, with the beautiful four mile valley, 800 feet wide and four miles long, lying before it.

In 1864, for the dedication, the Right Reverend Bishop Carroll, on horse back, was met by the young men from the parish, about three miles from the church. The congregation met them at the foot of the hill and formed a procession to the new church. Repeated discharges from a small cannon announced the glorious day to everyone in the valley. How fitting, that through the struggles and commitment of the settlers, the church of St. Joseph in the Hills sits like a crown on the top of God's Hill.

(Photo courtesy of photographer Frank Simkonis)

At the time of the dedication, many interior furnishings were missing. Through the untiring efforts of Father Schulte, everything was acquired. In 1864 a pipe organ was purchased for $1,060.00. A $500 gift from a parishioner and subscriptions made this possible. The beautiful high altar was also bought and paid for at this time.

With the church well porvided for they turned their attention to a new school.

After 17 years, the little log cabin Father Voll had built was much too small, plus the lay teachers who had taught through the 1850's had not been provided a home. It was decided to combine a school and teachers house in one structure.

Needed materials were hauled to the site and a stone building 48 X 26 was built that would serve the community well for 52 years.

St. Joseph Parochial School, Erected 1868

(Picture from Lonnie Enzweiler scrap book)

In 1868, the new school building was completed. One hundred fifty children attended St. Joseph School that year. School was taught in German, but some classes were in English.

Mike Enzweiler tells of his brother failing to put the emergency brake on when he parked his car. The car rolled down the drive into the school building. Since their father was a carpenter, he repaired the damage to the building.

When the church was completed and the new school was built, it would seem the little community could enjoy a time free of struggles and hardships. That joy, however, was short lived.

On March 20, 1870, the church was struck by lightning. The bolt entered the steeple, followed along the ceiling and descended on the main altar as far as the tabernacle containing the Blessed Sacrament. It glanced off the tabernacle and entered the ground by way of the rear wall. Fortunately there was no fire from the strike, but part of the steeple was destroyed along with part of the roof and ceiling. All of the windows were shattered.

It was a great calamity but proved, in a strange way, to be a blessing. The sympathy felt by all the local and city parishes for the struggling little parish at Four Mile led to a committee that solicited financial assistance. Funds came in abundantly. Not only was there enough to make all the necessary repairs, but there was a balance left for further reduction of the standing debt.

The balance of the century was spent building. A Pastors' residence was built in 1882. In 1888, the teachers' residence was converted into classrooms and a frame addition was added for a new residence.

In 1890, Sisters of Divine Providence came to teach in the school. It was the first parochial school taught by the sisters in America. They stayed for ten years. There are records of 45 students being taught by two nuns in one room!

The twentieth century brought beautiful stained glass windows to the church and seven murals painted in oils by Leon Lippert. It also saw a new school building which has been added to several times.

The new school was a two room frame building. The rooms became know as the "Big room" and the "Little Room". The distinction had nothing to do with size. Older students enjoyed the "Big Room" while younger students used the "little Room". Many remember two buckets of water with ladles sitting on the school steps. One was for adults and the other for the children.

I had a delightful chat with Dennis Walter and his 93 year old mother, Hilda Walter. This feisty animated lady told me about riding her horse on her daily four mile trip to school. Her horse spent the day in a stall in a barn located part way up the drive to the school. She recalls being in the play, *For Pete's Sake,* produced by her 8th grade class, and remembers music programs they prepared for the community to come to see.

This two room school has been enlarged several times. Modern restrooms and a kitchen have also been added.

Progress and perpetual motion are synonymous for these people. In Camp Springs at St. Joseph Church or St. Joseph School, if a need arises – they see it and they do it!

SUMMARY

When I started this project, I wanted to write about a community and a people I had developed a deep respect for. I discovered the book had already been written. It was written in fragments scattered in many places. I simply needed to find the segments and put them together in one place so the whole story could unfold.

It is a beautiful true story. A story of immigrants leaving their homeland to escape insurmountable problems, to find a new life, enduring hunger and the misery of the long journey to find freedom and opportunity. They asked for nothing more, in return, than a chance to work for their existence.

Now that the pieces are in one place I understand how clearly those early settlers are represented in the current population. The last names of the early settlers are generously represented in the current residents. What is extraordinary is the identical character of these people; the can-do spirit, the commitment and dedication to their church and their school. They are a perfect example of the patchwork that is America - a proud group of people committed to retaining the gift of community developed and passed on to them by their ancestors, moving forward but respecting their past.

There is an awareness that they are a living history, a continuation of the story of that beautiful hill that stands out in the rolling hills, as a special place. It is the silent ongoing acceptance of the stewardship of God's Hill.

POST SCRIPT

As the school year approached with fewer enrollments and rumors of school closing, I saw a dark shadow over my hopes to write a book about the history of this wonderful community that they could sell to bring in some revenue for the school. It is an inspiring story of a tiny group of people who refused to accept anything but success. I determined I would complete the book no matter what. It is a story that needs to be shared with the world.

I have to report, with heavy heart, part of the glorious history you have just read, has come to an end. In July, 2015 the powers that be, with equally heavy hearts, announced that after 164 years of beating all odds and prevailing over all challenges, St. Joseph School will not open in September.

The year I have spent researching this history, getting to know these people and their ancestors, makes it impossible for me to accept this as the final word. I feel they will, as in the past, find a way to turn this tremendous defeat into something positive for this inspiring little community. I have no way of knowing what that will be, but I am sure St. Joseph School will continue. The much needed pre-school will open this year. To that extent, St. Joseph School has a new beginning, a seed that may grow. I pray for their future, as the stewardship of God's Hill continues.

This Poem was written in the 1930's by Lee M. Trauth. It was found in the estate of a parishioner who passed away in 1983. I'm sure it has deep meaning to anyone who was fortunate enough to have experienced the loving education of St. Joseph School.

ST JOSEPH-in-the-Hills

Far from modern city rumble
Far from all industrial ills
Nestled in Kentucky's highlands
Stands St Joseph's in the hills.

Here its spire, a rigid finger
Pointing nobly heav'ns way
Beacons to the valley trav'ler
To ascend the hills and pray.

Steeped in love and old tradition
Standing here a hundred years
Landmark of a bygone era
Built by faithful stern pioneers.

Here they came with ax and plowshare
Tilled the valleys, bridged the rills
And with Christian faith and labor
Built St Joseph's in the hills.

Thus their church was interwoven
With their lives, and going their way
They left it to the generations-
Thus is stands...the same today.

And Oh! 'tis sacred when the sun sets
And a lonely cardinal trills
While the wind is whisp'ring softly
O'er St Joseph's in-the-hills

SPECIAL PEOPLE

These are the wonderful people who have shared their knowledge and memories with me. They are listed in the order they became involved in the writing of this book.

MIKE ENZWEILER - Mike has been my "first responder" during this entire project. If he didn't have the answer, he referred me to someone who did.

ERVIN ENZWEILER
LONNIE ENZWEILER
MELROSE GUTHIER
I met these three along with Mike at the Camp Springs Winery for our first meeting. They gave me information and stories about the history of the area. Lonnie also had a binder full of pictures, maps and clippings. Scans of some of these items along with items from Melrose are presented throughout the book to add visual clarity to the story.

DON BAUMANN - A true historian and expert genealogist, Don's research into the original settlers has been invaluable. His research has taken him to Germany to examine the records there showing when the settlers left their native land. The names, arrival dates and family information comes from his work.

MARK RAMLER - I needed information about the rock houses. Mike told me about Mark's book about them. I acquired the book and spoke to Mark on several occasions. He has provided information about the houses and has also allowed me to use some of his beautiful photographs of the properties in the book.

TIFFANY HOPPENJANS - Tiffany is the Curator of Exhibits and Collections at Behringer-Crawford Museum in Devou Park in Covington, KY. I heard the museum had in the past had an exhibit on wine making in the area. I made an appointment with Tiffany at the museum.

Tiffany had gathered the information that had been in the exhibit for me. Several of the papers I found there provided a wealth of material for the book.

NOTE: The Behringer-Crawford Museum is a beautiful little museum, packed with historical items from our local past and the views from Devou Park are a breath taking "must see."

DENNIS WALTER and his extra special mother, HILDA WALTER- They resolved several of my puzzles and added new anecdotes for the book. Sitting at the kitchen table, listening to her stories and memories was a total delight.

FRANK SIMKONIS – Award winning photographer. I saw photos he had taken for a program about Camp Springs. I wanted that beautiful view for the cover of the book. I called Frank Simkonis, who graciously gave me permission to use his pictures. The cover photo is from a beautiful panarama of the area. It provides a perfect picture of God's Hill.

KEITH NELTNER- Keith is a member of the Neltner family. He now owns the Baumann stone home and was a great help. I have wondered if the next generation will assume the role of stewards. Meeting this young man, with his eyes on the future and his heart in the past, I know God's Hill is in good hands.

CHRISTINE WAGNER-Christine is my very special editor who even managed to find in my sloppy notes enough information to create satisfactory End Notes which I had omitted.

My heartfelt thanks to everyone who has helped make this book a reality.

Works Cited

Alexander, Rachel "Preservation and Design Guidelines. "Bricks and Mortor: Thoughts on Historic Preservation, Community and Design. February 15, 2013. Word Press. Web

Baumann, Donald A. "Camp Springs, Kentucky: Historical insights" http://www.campsprings.com PDF file.Web

Baumann, Donald A. Personal correspondence 2015

Bell, Patricia "How to Build a Homemade Kiln Ehow. Demand media, 2015 Web

Bracke, Lisa, compiler, "St. Joseph's Catholic Church."Historical Facts" 2008 Microsoft Word File.

"Camp Springs.com" www.campsprings.com. Camp Springs Initiative. 1998 Web.

"Camp Springs House." Wikpedia. Wikimedia Foundation. Jan. 2015. Web

"Camp Springs Vineyard." *Campspringsvineyard Camp Springs Vineyard, 2015. Web.*

Commonwealth of Kentucky. Kentucky Historic Resources Survey. Baumann House .Kentucky History Council: CP-52. Print

Commonwealth of Kentucky. Kentucky Historic Resources Survey. Blau's Four Mile House. Kentucky History Council: CP-61. Print

Commonwealth of Kentucky. Kentucky Historic Resources Survey. Mathias Kremer House. Kentucky History Council: CP-59. Print

Commonwealth of Kentucky. *Kentucky Historic Resources Survey. Reitman House. Kentucky History Council: CP-78 Print*

Commonwealth of Kentucky. *Kentucky Historic Resources Survey. St. Joseph's Catholic Church. Kentucky History Council: CP-62 Print*

Crews, Ed. *"History.org: The Colonial Williamsburg Foundation official History and Citizenship website. "Making, Baking and Laying Bricks: The Colonial Williamsburg Official History and Citizenship site. The Colonial Williamsburg Foundation. Winter 2005-2006 Web*

Dee Andrea. *"Back to Their Roots: Northern Kentucky Wineries. "Northern Kentucky Heritage XIX-2: pg 19-25 Print*

Harding Laurie, editor. *The Camp Springs Press. Issue #3.pdf. Web*

Kentucky Wine. Kentucky Wine, 2013. Kentucky Grape and Wine Council. Web

Neltner's Farm, Camp Springs, Kentucky. "Neltner's Farm, Neltner's Farm LLC, 2004. Web

"New Film Showcases Kentucky Wines, New York Times 21 May 2007 late ed: A1, Print

Plattner Elisa "Architecture as a Cultural Artifact." Included in display at Behringer-Crawford Museum. Personal interaction 2015

StoneBrook Winery. *StoneBrook Winery* 2015 Web

www.ingramcontent.com/pod-product-compliance
Lightning Source LLC
Chambersburg PA
CBHW041528090426
42736CB00036B/231